RECOGNIZING THE

LOVE TRAP

Dr. Rhonda Smith

ND, BCALP

ACKNOWLEDGMENTS

After the completion of my book *Stop the Storm Now: Rise and Walk In Your Divine Purpose!*, The Lord revealed to me my assignment was still incomplete. He placed a calling on my life to enlighten those struggling with addictive behaviors, whether physical or emotional, as to why they seek out and engage in activities/relationships even though they are causing them harm. Once equipped with the insight behind the "Why" of a destructive behavior, we are better prepared to change that behavior altogether.

In Recognizing the Love Trap, my objective is to prevent others from continuously slipping into the same toxic patterns, and disastrous relationships. I, myself, was a victim of a vicious cycle of repeatedly falling for the same type of narcissistic person that drained my energy and destroyed my joy. When I finally learned why, with God's help I was able to confront and destroy the reasons I was settling for less than I am worthy of.

This book ministers to anyone that has ever been in an addictive relationship with an individual or a substance. Allow it to help heal the past, and prepare you for a brighter future. I thank God He helped me stop dating Bozo's, so He could prepare me for my Boaz!

Special thanks to God for enlightening me to the dream. To my grandson Terrance Junior who is my awesome graphic designer. To my daughter Tamika, my son-in-law Terrance Senior, and my mother for being supportive. Finally, thank you Ross Rosenberg, my mentor and friend!

TABLE OF CONTENTS

Chapter 1: The Beginning of a Toxic Relationship 1

Trauma Attachment...1

CODEPENDENCY 2

Trauma Bonding...3

Cognitive Dissonance 4

Why You Stay..6

Chapter 2: The Roles within a Toxic Relationship...................8

The Codependent Party..8

Symptoms of Codependency 10

Bounded by Their Wounds 12

The Codependent & Narcissist Dance 15

The Narcissist Party 17

The Continuum of Self Scale 20

CODEPENDENT CONTINUUM..21

NARCISSIST CONTINUUM 23

Chapter 3: The Stages of a Toxic Relationship 25

Honeymoon/Idealization Stage 25

The First Red Flag Stage...25

The Promise To Do Better Stage...26

The Blame Game Stage...26

Walking on Egg-shells Stage...27

The Isolation Stage 27

The Desperation Stage 27

Experiencing the Stages...28

Chapter 4: Are You in a Toxic Relationship 31

Awareness 31

Embarrassment..32

Pathological Loneliness 33

Triggers..35

Was it Really that Bad? 36

Six Dangerous Signs that You are in a Toxic Relationship 37

Chapter 5: Breaking Free from a Toxic Relationship...........39

My Own Breakthrough..39

Seven Steps to Breaking Free...41

CHAPTER 1: THE BEGINNING OF A TOXIC RELATIONSHIP

Trauma Attachment

Attachment is the emotional bond that typically forms between infant and caregiver. Attachment is cultivated during a critical period of development; during the years of infancy, childhood, and adolescence. The expectations that are formed during these periods tend to remain relatively unchanged for the rest of the person's life and becomes the blue print for their future relationships. Attachment, or lack thereof, affects everything from our partner selection to how well our relationships progress, and sadly to how they end. That's why recognizing our attachment pattern can help us understand our strengths and vulnerabilities in a relationship.

When there is a secure attachment pattern, a person is confident and is able to easily interact with others, meeting both their own and another's needs. Securely attached adults tend to be more satisfied in their relationships. Their relationship tends to be honest, open and equal, with both people feeling independent, yet loving toward each other.

Unlike securely attached individuals, people with an insecure attachment tend to be desperate to form a fantasy bond. Instead of feeling real love or trust toward their partner, they often feel emotional hunger. They're constantly looking to their partner to rescue or complete them. They fulfill their need of safety and security by clinging to their partner, and sometimes being demanding or possessive.

Insecure attachment happens when parents cannot give their child the feeling of security that he or she needs. Usually, this happens completely unintentionally. Substance abuse, depression, stress, anxiety, frequent moves, separation from a primary caregiver, physical and/or emotional neglect, an inexperienced mother, sexual abuse, as well as domestic violence are all factors that can hinder secure attachment. Many of these are generational. They become so familiar, they're not recognized as dysfunction. How many of us grew up experiencing at least one, if not all of these on a regular basis? This Attachment Trauma is the beginning of a downward spiral..

We must stop blaming our parents for something they were never taught to do. Our graves are rich with our ancestors' dreams. I'm sure they would have hoped they could have been courageous and learned about this painful bondage. I'm sure they would have wanted to do something about this crippling silent curse that is destroying our loved ones. We must educate ourselves so we can put a halt to this epidemic. It's so important that you have the right resources so that you can learn how to be loved and how to love without the dysfunction.

CODEPENDENCY

Those of us who have suffered from some form of trauma attachment as children, as adults seek high levels of intimacy, responsiveness and approval from partners and become overly dependent. Codependency is a learned behavior that can be passed down from one generation to another. It is also known as "Relationship Addiction" because codependents often form or maintain relationships that are one-sided, emotionally destructive and/or abusive.

Codependency is about over-functioning in someone else's life but under-functioning in your own. It involves sacrificing your personal needs to try to meet the needs of others. Codependency usually draws an individual into relationships with others who demand love, respect and care, but who cannot give the same back.

Codependents often get in abusive relationships in which they dismiss the abuse because they are so dependent on the other person for the emotional nurturing they never got as a child, even though these partners are often emotionally unavailable like one or both of their parents or guardians were. Narcissists are considered to be natural magnets for the codependent. I will expound on this later in the book.

As a child, codependent behaviors can be necessary for survival. However, in adulthood, these behaviors can prevent a person from developing truly stable relationships. As a consequence of growing up in a dysfunctional family environment, codependents often suffer further trauma due to relationships with people who may be abandoning, abusive, addicted or have mental illness.

Trauma Bonding

Trauma Bonding is defines as a bond that forms due to intense, emotional experiences, usually with a toxic person. This is similar to Stockholm Syndrome. It is the condition that causes a hostage to develop a physiological alliance with their kidnappers during captivity. In a similar way, we are held emotional captive to the manipulator or narcissist.

Trauma Bonding is like an addictive drug. A psychologically abusive relationship that is like a rollercoaster, with punishment during times of disapproval and the intermittent reinforcement of kindness when you behave. The physical body is going through its own turmoil; with high levels of stress hormones countered by dopamine when given affection as a reward.

This hormonal roller coaster really takes its toll on somebody's body. Sometimes people experience headaches, chest pain, and even autoimmune disorders .Victims stay in these relationships despite the stress on their anatomy. This back-and-forth negative and positive reinforcement causes the body to become addicted.

Cognitive Dissonance

Due to addiction, *Cognitive Dissonance* is also how we become bond to a toxic relationship. This term is used to describe the feelings of discomfort that results when your beliefs does not support your behavior. For example, it is as being addicted to cigarettes. Yes, we know that smoking (behavior) is bad for our health and our beliefs concerning smoking conflicts with the practice. However, we are addicted to the cigarette and continue—all while knowing that it's against our best interest.

We as humans do not always like this inner conflict. So we wish to restore harmony regardless if our reality really is pleasant or not. For instance, if our comfortable beliefs or perspectives are challenged, we experience cognitive dissonance as an intense feeling of discomfort, but with a very strong urge to restore harmony. Many times, we prefer to get back to the harmony stage instead of making changes and solving the problem. To create this harmony, many smokers often say, "Well I have to die from something!"

Cognitive Dissonance is a psychological term that also describes the uncomfortable tension that victims experience when in a relationship with a narcissist. It is a common defense mechanism that the victim uses to cope with the deception, domination, and abuse that occurs in the relationship. This helps them stay in a dysfunctional relationship instead of dealing with the fear of being alone. Perhaps you have heard such a coping mechanism such as, "Well the grass isn't always greener on the other side!"

As you can imagine, this tension is mind blowing and throws the victim into many inner conflicts and defense mechanism; cognitive dissonance being one. For example, a women who is abused by her pathological narcissist spouse will hate the conditions she is living in. However, with the fear of being alone and the trauma bonding that has formed, she will rationalize and tell herself, "He only fights me because he loves her." This inner dialogue reduces her anxiety and allows her to bond.

Why You Stay

Keep in mind, codependency and narcissism is not gender specific. Either party can be male or female. Being so, the question is always, "Why does she stay?" or "Why does he stay?" This is often the first question that comes to mind when someone hears of a bad outcome between a victim and his/her harsh mate. They wonder why she decided to stay with the person who demonstrated a pattern of unstable and vile behavior. For the outsider, it looks like a simple and logical answer to walk away from anyone who poses a threat of causing anyone psychological damage. Nevertheless, the reasons many stay in entangled and harmful relationships are more complex. Bonding is not always a synonym for love and chemistry can be extremely strong even with the wrong person.

As with all psychological symptoms, there are underlying brain functions that are responsible for this behavior. Two of the most prominent neurochemicals that are linked to traumatic bonding are dopamine and oxytocin. The imbalance of chemistry can cause the victim to experience intense cravings of wanting her partner. Being so, the brain's reward system is often the motivation behind a victim's decision to stay. Unfortunately ,this has led to the negative consequences for many victims—some who have lost their lives. This combination of neurochemistry can create an addictive attachment that is difficult to break. I work with many addictions. Addictions as: heroin, crack fentanyl, alcohol and most of them say that codependency addiction is far harder to break.

In extreme cases, people use drugs in relationships to reduce their anxiety so that they can function. This is when a person is trying to manage a strong emotion that can be overwhelming. Most people that are addicted to drugs or a narcissistic relationship do have trauma that has happened in their childhood (attachment trauma); so they regulate this reality with a drug and sometimes the drug is the relationship.

Because the pain is so unbearable, a lot of times, we disconnect from ourselves so that we don't have to feel the pain of devastation. We live a life of lies. We are caught up in a web of deception. We make up excuses for this mistreatment so that we don't have to be alone. It's Explosive! You try to make some sense out of this craziness. You become bonded to the very thing you should have let go. Now you see how it all begins; to early childhood trauma attachment, leading to codependency, then falling into trauma bonding and then finally cognitive dissonance. Against your better judgment, you have become addicted. This is why you stay.

Chapter 2: The Roles within a Toxic Relationship

The Codependent Party

One of the two roles within a toxic relationship is the **Codependent Party**. As we discuss the codependent, have you ever heard the term *Codependent Behavior*? Many of us may have used this term in our casual conversations. We have seen it being used both correctly and incorrectly. As a society, we assume this term is no more harmful than a person being needy so we dangerously miss how serious this addiction can be. Many of us quickly excuse ourselves from ever suffering from this relationship addiction and argue that we can live in 100% happiness without a mate. But we would be surprised how the little things we casually do are often tendencies of co-dependent behavior.

We may have all seen our friends call their mate 20 times a day, stalk them during their lunch hour or discourage them from having other friends. Although this behavior is so common that it seems normal, these are tendencies toward an unhealthy addictive relationship. More often than not, when we talk about this dysfunction, our knowledge is usually based out of something we read, saw or heard about. It is rare that we use it to describe what we have done and the mistakes that we have made. But according to an article in the New York Times, 96% percent of all Americans have suffered from codependent behavior more than once in our life.

Being codependent is usually based out of the habits we developed in our childhood. For example, we have a great need to please others and be accepted, so we learn quickly to satisfy other people's needs before we consider our own. We fulfill what they want, before we consider what we want. After a while, pleasing others before pleasing ourselves becomes a way of life. It becomes our new normal. In fact, when we are tempted to fulfill a personal desire we want, early in life, we start thinking that we are being selfish and unfair. This habit-forming addiction quickly seeps into our adult years and it becomes simply the way we behave with others. In fact, the more we blindly give to others, the easier it becomes.

Being that we are creatures of habit, our need for acceptance often becomes stronger once we realize what it means to be rejected. We don't understand that rejection is God's protection. So instead of becoming wiser and more level-headed in our later years, we find that we become addicted and therefore go deeper and deeper into this maze of blindly giving. Many experts say that being codependent is being in an one-sided relationship. Regardless if this is something that you contend with on a regular basis or not, most of us can relate to being in a relationship where we felt used, under-appreciated, and taken for granted. Deep down you knew the reason you kept accepting the harsh treatment; it is based out of the fear of being alone! The reward of selling out your own wishes for them is so that they will talk to you, interact with you, and acknowledge you. Another word for Codependency is SLDD which stands for Self-Love Deficit Disorder (Ross Rosenberg). This is an addiction that is more painful and worse than any other addiction.

As mentioned in the Chapter 1 *Codependency* section, codependence is a person who is in a relationship that gives a great deal of love, respect and care in hopes that this is going to be mutual and reciprocal within the partnership. When it is not, they will continue to stay in the relationship even if they don't receive back the love, respect and care. Recognizing these signs of codependency is very difficult. Normally, a trauma or separation has to happen to be able to detect this behavior.

Codependents often get in abusive relationships in which they dismiss the abuse because they are so dependent on the other person for the emotional nurturing they never got as a child. Often, a child grows up in a home where their emotions are ignored or punished. This emotional neglect can give the child low self-esteem and shame. They may believe their needs are not worth attending to.

Symptoms of Codependency

• **Low Self-Esteem:** Codependency may cause feelings of shame and worthlessness. A person may believe they do not deserve happiness. If a person does not value themselves, they may try to get others to value them. The sense of "being needed" can prompt internal gratification, even if the recipient of care does not show gratitude.

• **Poor Boundaries:** Codependent people often feel responsible for others' happiness. They can have a hard time saying "no" or putting their own needs first. They may hide their true thoughts and feelings to avoid upsetting others.

• **A Need to "Save" Others:** Codependent people may feel it is their duty to protect their loved ones from all harm. If a loved one does something wrong, they will likely try to fix the situation on loved one's behalf. Such behavior can prevent others from becoming independent or learning from their mistakes. It may also enable abuse or addiction to persist unchallenged.

• **Self-Denial:** A codependent person often prioritizes others' well-being over their own. They may deny their own needs for rest, emotional support, and self-care. They may feel guilt or anxiety when asserting their own desires. Codependent people can feel uneasy when others offer support.

• **Perfectionism:** Codependent people often project an image of self-reliance and competence. It is common for people to take on more responsibilities than they can handle.

• **Control Issues:** A codependent person may link their own self-worth to others' well-being. If a loved one fails, a codependent person may feel as if they failed themselves. Their attempts to make others' lives better may shift into controlling or possessive behavior.

When I realized that I was codependent, I kept saying there is no way I could be codependent. What I did not understand is that this is an emotional bondage and not a physical one. You may look good on the outside, but there is something deeper brewing on the inside. I am so happy

God anointed, appointed and commissioned me to be transparent and tell the truth. You have to be honest with yourself, be courageous and take a deep reflection. View the codependent symptoms carefully to determine if you are the particular party within a toxic relationship.

Bounded by Their Wounds

As stated earlier, generally there is an involuntary attraction between codependents and narcissists. (It's very important to note that neither condition is gender specific. A narcissist can be a man or a woman, and likewise a codependent can be a man or a woman.) They are drawn to each other like a magnet. This gravitational pull to one another stems from their childhood wounds. They both suffer from attachment trauma, but the narcissist's wounds are more severe. The narcissist tends to be more angry and aggressive because of the treatment they sustained as a child. All children want their parents' approval and attention. Children adapt to their homes, and often the most reasonable adaptation to some home situations is to become a narcissist. We will soon discuss the role of the narcissist, but let us first consider the early childhood factors of a narcissist.

Narcissism Early childhood risk factors includes:

- Insensitive parenting.

- Abuse.

- Unpredictable or negligent care.

- Excessive criticism, a very domineering and devaluing parent who is always putting down the child, and has unrealistically high expectations.

- Trauma.

- Over-praising and excessive pampering—when parents focus intensely on a particular talent or the physical appearance of their child as a result of their own self-esteem issues.

Over-praising involves a parent who constantly praises a child and protects them from experiencing failure. When the child does fall short, the parent blames someone or something else. The child grows with a sense of entitlement and becomes convinced they are inherently special, feelings that can later manifest as narcissistic.

On the other hand, neglectful parenting, where the child is ignored or actively criticized, can lead to a situation where a child is constantly trying to prove the neglectful parent wrong. The child learns to cope with the parent's rejection by convincing themselves of being special and important. The constant desire to avoid being a loser can also manifest as narcissism later in life.

When a child is raised in a family that is very competitive and only rewards high achievement, love is conditional. Children in these families do not feel stably loved. They only feel secure and worthwhile when they are successful and recognized as the "best." The conditional love of their childhood and the over evaluation of high status and success in their home, sets in motion a lifelong pattern of chasing success and confusing it with happiness. Children who grow up in these households feel angry, humiliated, and inadequate. They are likely to react to their childhood situation in a few different ways.

Defeated: Some of these children simply give up and accept defeat. In their teenage years, after decades of being told that they are worthless, they may spiral down into a self-hating shame-based depression. Then to escape their inner shame, they may try to lose themselves in impulsive, addictive behaviors. Some become alcoholics and drug addicts .They never achieve their potential because they have been convinced that they have none.

Rebellious: These children overtly reject their parents' message that they are "losers." Instead, they spend their life trying to prove to themselves, the world, and the devaluing parent that they are special. They pursue achievement in every way that they can. Proving they are special becomes a lifelong mission, while underneath there is always a harsh inner voice criticizing their every mistake.

Angry: These children grow up furious at the devaluing parent. Anyone who reminds them of their parent in any way becomes the target of their anger. They sometimes become Toxic or Malignant themselves. It is not enough for them to achieve, they must destroy as well.

Knowing the traumatic experiences the now adult narcissist has lived through, it's no wonder they have an inflated sense of their own importance, a deep need for excessive attention and admiration, troubled relationships, and a lack of empathy for others. But behind this mask of extreme confidence lies a fragile self-esteem that's vulnerable to the slightest criticism.

The Codependent & Narcissist Dance

The naturally dysfunctional "Codependency Dance" requires two opposite partners: the pleaser/fixer (codependent) and the taker/controller (narcissist/addict). The narcissist is attracted to the codependent who feels perfect to them because they are allowed to take the lead which makes them feel powerful, competent, and appreciated.

Codependents who are giving, sacrificing, and consumed with the needs and desires of others, do not know how to avoid romantic relationships with individuals who are selfish, self-centered, controlling, and harmful to them. As natural followers in their relationship dance, codependents are passive and accommodating dance partners. They find narcissistic dance partners deeply appealing. They are perpetually attracted to their charm, boldness, confidence and domineering personality.

When codependents and narcissists pair up, the dancing experience sizzles with excitement — at least in the beginning. However, after many "songs," the thrilling dance experience transforms into drama, conflict, feelings of neglect and being trapped. Even with chaos and conflict, neither of the two spellbound dancers dares to end their partnership.

When a codependent and narcissist come together in their relationship, their dance unfolds flawlessly: Their roles seem natural to them because they have actually been practicing them their whole lives. The codependent reflexively gives up their power; since the narcissist thrives on control and power, the dance is perfectly coordinated. No one gets their toes stepped on.

A common misconception is that narcissists go for the weak, because they are easier to manipulate. In fact, narcissists prefer to try and hook someone who is strong-willed, and who has talents or characteristics they admire. This is because they see it as a challenge, and will find more entertainment in taking down someone impressive. They are also attracted to people who reflect well on themselves. They like to show off their partner in public, but abuse them behind the scenes. Ultimately, it's all about control.

Codependents confuse caretaking and sacrifice with loyalty and love. They are proud of their dedication to the person they love, but end up feeling used and unappreciated. Codependents consistently choose a partner to whom they are initially attracted, but will eventually resent. They are resistant to leaving their partner because of their lack of self-esteem. Their fear of being alone, and compulsion to fix the relationship at any cost, is often an extension of their yearning to be loved, respected, and cared for as a child. Although codependents dream of an unconditionally loving partner, they submit to their dysfunctional destiny until they decide to heal the psychological wounds that ultimately compel them to pick the narcissist.

You can make significant strides in overcoming consistently choosing the wrong dance partner by developing new attitudes, skills, and behavior. But deeper recovery truly involves healing trauma that usually began in childhood. Healing trauma is like going back in time. It requires reopening old wounds, cleaning them, and getting acquainted with missing parts of yourself. Facing what happened is the first step in healing.

Nearly everyone knows a friend or family member who continuously falls for unavailable partners or toxic relationships. While the solution may seem simple—that they should just leave—if we understood what makes people stay, it would build empathy and strengthen support at a time when that loved one may need it most.

The Narcissist Party

The second role within a toxic relationship is the **Narcissist Party**. The Narcissist has usually mastered the art of manipulation and takes full advantage of the *Codependent Party*. If only this victim understood that there are researched manipulation tactics that are discussed by the most respected experts on addiction. It might be easier for them to believe that the abuse that they are intertwined in has not affected millions of other people. Too many of them believe that no one truly understands their love chaos and that they are all alone. Once the victim realizes that what they consider as normal is actually a manipulation tactic, they will realize that many people have overcome the same web of addiction. Furthermore, others have learned to live a healthy and happy life with someone else; and they can too.

Lying is also one of the most used and easiest practiced manipulation tactics. Unfortunately, it is not looked at as being dangerous because it is a practice that everyone participates in during sometime in their lives. Unfortunately, it is normal to lie. The interesting thing about being addicted to a toxic relationship is that the entire foundation is built on a lie. For example, the abuser said that they adore you and is in love when they really aren't. The narcissist will tell roleplay any prolonged lie to get what they want.

Mood Swings is another tactic. The swinging of the narcissist moods keeps the victim on guard at all times. This can increase the victim's overall fear because from day to day, they don't know what the temperament of their mate will be. You don't know who your partner is from one moment to another. This is similar to the famous story of Dr. Jekyll or Mr. Hyde. He was one person, but had a personality that alternated between good and very evil.

Love Bombing is a Narcissist's Secret Weapon. This can be very tragic and emotional. Love bombing is the practice of over whelming someone with signs of adoration and attraction. When someone tells you they love you and how special you are, it can be intoxicating ,at first. Once they have you convinced, they will shape you into a member of their supporting cast. Narcissists move quickly to avoid detection.

The Silent Treatment is something mostly all of us are familiar with. This usually happens when we disapprove of something someone has done. Narcissists purposefully punish with the tactic of the silent treatment—it is used to teach the person it is directed at a lesson. Please know this punishment is used throughout the entire relationship. If you choose to stick around it will keep coming - until the often inevitable discard. The Narcissists will have you dangling until you die if you don't get out. And the longer they don't talk to you the deeper the manipulation.

Gaslighting is to manipulate someone by psychological means to the point they begin to question their own sanity. This manipulative mind and behavior control strategy is used to take control over a weak and defenseless victims. The abuser tricks the victim into believing that they are not mentally or emotionally stable. They manipulate them to the point that they don't trust their own judgement anymore. This results in the victim depending more and more on the abuser. When a person lies for their own gain to another person, so repeatedly and with so much confidence, the victim now begins to doubt her own soundness. The victim is now uncertain that she can perceive reality correctly and becomes dependent on the manipulator more than ever. This is exactly what the pathological narcissist wants.

Triangulation is when the abuser starts turning everyone against you. Many of times, this will result with your own family starting to wonder if you are in your "right mind". The reason narcissist do this is to get all of your attention to themselves. They want to make sure they turn people against you while they're also turning you against those people. The name of the game is to isolate you so that no one can tell you the truth about what is being done. Your mind is already mangled with lies. You believe whatever they say—all because you want to believe the fantasy and illusion you're in. Besides, it's too painful to accept the truth.

I'm going to give an example. I was dating a guy and he didn't like any of my friends. He would always say, "They are all jealous of you! You have a big fine home, fine cars, and money to travel around the world. You think they like that?" The reality was that he was afraid of what my friends would see in him; because deep down he couldn't understand why I was even dating him due to his own insecurities. Concerning the narcissist, they are very insecure.

Another example, I have a friend that I became close to. When I started educating her on this narcissistic syndrome she was very surprised. She thanked me because she realize that there was some familiar dynamics. Once her husband found out that I was educating her on this epidemic, he made sure that he put a halt to our friendship. She did just what he wanted. You see some people will stay entangled the rest of their lives. It's painful to take off the mask and breath because you might just be liberated. You're so use to holding your breath until you die. It has become your normal. But what about your children? Is this what you want for them—lies and deception? This can very well evolve into a generational curse.

The Continuum of Self Scale

Before you understand what has you bound, you have to understand what type of toxic individual you are entangled with and what part of the Self-Continuum Scale you and your mate fit into.

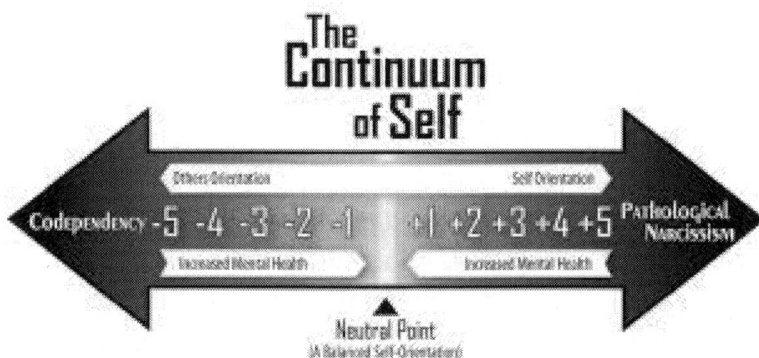

The Continuum Scale (CSV) is important to understand. The lower the CVS number, the more codependent you are. However, the higher your CVS the more narcissistic you are. The better chance of the SLD (Self-Love Deficit Disorder) known as *Codependency*. The other end of the spectrum explains the Pathological Narcissistic known as the *Emotional Manipulator*. Look at the following to see were you fall on the CVS scale. For more details on Ross Rosenberg "Continuum of Self Scale".

CODEPENDENT CONTINUUM

- 5 CSV: The codependent is completely absorbed with the ***Love, Respect and Care*** (LRC) needs of others, while completely ignoring and devaluing their own. This category of individual is often powerless, unable or unwilling to seek LRC from his/her romantic partner. This is the most extreme case of codependency.

- 4 CSV: The codependent is mostly absorbed with the LRC of others, but not completely. Almost always focused on the LRC needs of others while only intermittently seeking to have their own LRC needs reciprocated or fulfilled.

- 3 CSV: The codependent identifies with their caring and giving nature. He/she is predominantly focused on the LRC needs of others, while often diminishing, delaying or excusing away the fulfillment of their own needs. This person's identity is typically in relationships in which there is an imbalance in giving between his/her partner—all while giving much more LRC to their partner than receiving. This individual is capable of setting boundaries in relationships; while also asking for what he or she needs. However, he/she tends to feel guilty when setting such boundaries or when asking for help from the other party.

- 2 CSV: The codependent is able to set boundaries and ask for what they need when the LRC balance goes beyond their comfort level. They might experience mild feelings of guilt or neediness when asking their partner to meet their LRC needs. As much as possible he/she avoids individuals who are narcissistic, exploitative or manipulative.

-1 CVS: A codependent with the healthy balance between love, respect and care for self and others. They typically seeks life experiences and relationships in which they are able to satisfy their own LRC needs. They often enjoys caring for others, but this does not identify them as a caretaker or helper. They do not experience guilt or feelings of neediness when asking for LRC from their partner.

0 CVS: A person who participates in relationships where there is an equal distribution of LRC given and received. They easily ask for what they need from their partners, while being open to their partners LRC needs. With their LRC-balanced relationship, they easily fluctuate between being the recipient and giver of LRC.

NARCISSIST CONTINUUM

+1 CVS: A person with a healthy balance between love, respect and care for self and others. They tend to participate and appreciate relationships that are based on reciprocal in mutual distribution of LRC.

+2 CVS: A person who prefers to be involved in relationships in which the pursuit to fulfill his ambitions, desires and goals are encouraged and supported. Although he/she is a go-getter and may be consumed with getting the spotlight, he/she is willing and able to fulfill his/her partner's needs. He/she is neither explorative nor selfish.

+3 CVS: A mildly selfish and self-centered individual. He/she is typically in relationships where there is an imbalance in the distribution of LRC needs, expecting or taking more LRC than giving. If confronted about the LRC inequality, he/she may get defensive, but will be able to make corrections.

+4 CVS: A narcissistic individual. This person is self-absorbed and preoccupied with the LRC needs of self, while rarely seeking to fulfill the LRC needs of others. He/she comes across as being entitled and self-centered. Although this person is overtly narcissistic, he/she is still able to give nominal levels of LRC to others. If confronted about the LRC inequalities, he/she will characteristically get angry and defensive and is quick to justify his/her actions. However, they do not exhibit narcissistic rage when confronted.

+5 CVS: A pathological narcissist is unable and unmotivated to love, respect or care for others. He/she is consumed with fulfilling his/her LRC needs with no intention of reciprocating it. He/she has great difficulty in exhibiting empathy and unconditional love. When he/she does give LRC to others, it is usually conditional with arrangements or strings attached. He/she is not able to see or comprehend their pathological levels of narcissism. When confronted about the LRC imbalances, he/she will often strike back with either direct or passive aggression (Rage).

CHAPTER 3: THE STAGES OF A TOXIC RELATIONSHIP

Honeymoon/Idealization Stage

In the beginning, everything is just like in the movies. They smile, you smile, and the fireworks fly. When you meet they are charming, making you feel singled out and special. You feel like soul-mates as if you've known each other for years. They put you on a pedestal by focusing on your strengths and capabilities. They're so easy to talk to that they draw out your deepest fears and insecurities. The relationship moves quickly by texts, calls and meetings. They'll say you're kind, generous and trusting, unlike their ex who was greedy, selfish and untrustworthy, or bipolar.

The First Red Flag Stage

This is the stage where you're starting to see those things that are going to be big problems later on. You're still convincing yourself that the relationship isn't serious enough yet to worry about it, or that love can conquer all. There are occasional criticisms and put-downs, as well as unexpected anger and mood swings that leave you thrown off course. They start questioning your looks, friendships and choice of career. There is also sometimes jealous behavior, condescending remarks, and cruel jokes to humiliate you in public. When you protest they tell you to lighten up, and that you can't take a joke.

The Promise To Do Better Stage

All those little warnings signs have become indicators of doom. You've had your first big fight (or three) and you're thinking it's time to get out before you get any more attached. But then it happens. He/she apologizes. They tell you they know what they've done is bad, but they can do better. They *will* do better. They've finally realized what you mean to them and how you're the best thing that's ever happened. They promise everything will be great from here on out.

The Blame Game Stage

Shocker: That promise didn't last very long. You're holding on, and you don't even remember why. You're fighting the same fights over and over, and no matter how many times he promises, it doesn't change. So you figure the problem must be with you. They blame and accuse, saying it's all your fault. When you try to justify, argue, defend, and explain, they say you're just being jealous, you're lying, or stupid. And if you get upset they say you're crazy. They see-saw between nice and nasty to keep you off balance. They tell you they are disappointed and you're not the person they thought you were, to make you jump through hoops for their approval.

You may find out they've been lying in this stage but you turn a blind eye believing it was all for your own good. You focus on their good behavior, and when it's bad you become a master at sweeping it under the carpet.

Walking on Egg-shells Stage

In this stage, you are expected to be a mind reader, a tower of strength, and a never-ending source of love and adoration. You try to control people, places, things and events to keep from upsetting them. You're unable to be spontaneous, so you plan everything in advance. And you keep secrets and lie to your family and friends.

The Isolation Stage

They isolate you from family and friends by either overtly lying on them, or turning people against you behind your back . They may reveal your deepest secrets, or fake concern to loved ones that you're not mentally stable, or that you're having affairs. They may even accuse YOU of being abusive. You avoid family and friends to keep the peace, spending time either with or waiting for the abuser. Spending time with others is no longer fun as he/she monitors your time by constantly texting and giving you the third degree afterwards. You seek escape routes through alcohol, food, drugs, or shopping.

The Desperation Stage

In this stage, the narcissist may use anger, ramp up the silent treatment, or do a disappearing act. They may also be less willing to hide having an affair by flaunting photos of their latest flame on social media. You feel utterly hopeless, alone and invisible. You may suffer from depression, anxiety and fatigue.

Feeling that you've had enough and can't take anymore, you may threaten to leave, try to get counselling or even seriously contemplate suicide. They may discard you at this point, leaving you alone and feeling helpless. Or they realize that you've had enough and move back to stage one, the honeymoon/hope phase. Again, they promise to change, stop drinking, raging and start being the person you used to know and love. They may even suggest going for couple counselling. But somehow it always ends up the same. Time and time again. Year after year. Until you wonder what happened to you, and your life. Even if you break up it's usually not quite the end. These relationships are intense, and you may find yourself cycling through the stages, and going through several breakups and makeups before it ends for good.

Experiencing the Stages

Within my toxic relationship, I've been through the honey moon stage. I can describe this as falling in love quick, fast and in a hurry. Only wanting to be around this person while thinking that he was my soul-mate. In the beginning, he will place me on a peddle-stool and flourish me with compliments. Did he mean it? Viewing the *Continuum of Self Scale*, the man in this relationship I will categorize as a **+4 CVS** on the *Narcissist Continuum*. Go back and read the description. This man was a narcissistic individual, but he was not a pathological narcissist. To answer the question, a person in this category may very well mean the kind things they say. Now a pathological narcissist (liar) **+5 CVS** doesn't, but someone who is borderline just might mean the compliments they say. They really think they love you, but just simply have abandonment issues. On the other hand, a pathological narcissist is heartless.

While dating the narcissist individual, I was a **-3 CVS** on the *Codependency Continuum*. Even though I had boundaries, I was still attracted to this person. However, there was a red flag. I couldn't pinpoint any solid evidence, but my intuition was telling me that this should not have been. Nothing that I knew for certain, but there was something that I knew was wrong.

Concerning the narcissist promising to do better, this is not a promise that will always come because sometimes, they won't have a clue. This is because they don't see that they did anything wrong. To be honest, they will want you to do better.

Then comes the blame-game. I heard things like, "You just crazy. Everything is your fault, if you just act right and do right!" Everything that is wrong with them they will project on you.

Sooner than later, it was as I was walking on egg-shells. One scenario I remember was always making sure that I didn't trigger that little boy on the inside. For instance, anything that he wanted to do that I didn't was an explosive fallout. This included us always hanging around other people. The narcissist is more concerned about the perception of others; this is because they have a false identity.

This brings us to the isolation stage of my experience. I know that he was isolating me because he didn't want others to see the reality of the relationship. This man will purposefully and intentionally place negative ideas within my mind concerning my friends and family.

I have dated both the narcissist individual **+4 CVS** and the pathological narcissist **+5 CVS**. When I finally said that I have had enough, this brought the relationships to the desperation stage. Now this is not to say that the codependent is becoming desperate, but it is rather the narcissist party who reaches to desperate measures—all because they do not want you to leave. They become desperate to try to keep you.

There is a major difference here with the narcissist individual and the pathological narcissist. The narcissist individual may be selfish and self-centered, but his intention is not to hurt you; even during his desperation. On the other hand the pathological narcissist goal is to hurt you. For example, the narcissist will cheat, but try hide it. The pathological narcissist will put it right in your face. It is the craziest thing ever.

When the pathological narcissist I broke up with entered into the desperation stage, it was as he was trying to brain wash me. His approach was to be direct with his cheating and use it to make me jealous. He even sent me a text message picture of a half-naked woman saying, "This is who I'm with right now." He will later call saying things like, "That's why I'm not with you right now!" The goal was for me to be overwhelmed with jealousy and insecurities and go running back. Don't fall into the trap.

CHAPTER 4: ARE YOU IN A TOXIC RELATIONSHIP

Awareness

It is so interesting, but for most of us, it is much easier to give an opinion and comment correctly on the problems of someone else relationship problems than our own! Although this is not often discussed, the more emotionally attached we are to the person in the relationship, the more likely our assessment is correct and point on!

What I am saying is if your daughter came to you because of unhealthy attachment issues, many times you would be able to explore with her why she has these issues, when the issues started, and what she need to do to fix her self-worth issues. It is funny because when it comes to our own complex attachment issues we instantly have blinders on.

This is why the first step of realizing that you are in a toxic relationship is awareness. To be honest, some people just live there. They never seem to discover why they keep on going back.

Well, the question is, "How do we become aware of a toxic relationship?" From experience, I can tell you that you have to hit rock-bottom first! The pain has to become so bad that we have no choice but to take the blinders off. This awareness even allows our eyes to be open to the pattern of how we choose a partner. This is when we want to know what's wrong and why we keep on choosing the same kind of person.

Embarrassment

When a victim is aware that they are finally in a toxic relationship, sooner or later, they are unable to hide this reality from family and friends. Their depth of their suffering becomes even more intense and personal. It is common for the victim to initially experience feelings of embarrassment. This feeling comes because their family and friends now know that they have allowed themselves to get wrapped up tightly in a relationship of lies.

When their feelings become overwhelmingly embarrassing, the embarrassment quickly develops into paranoia. They believe that people are looking, laughing and judging their every move; even when they are not. They also start believing that their actions look more magnified and extreme than what they actually are. They don't realize that their loved ones are not judging one single behavior, but instead they are concerned with the victim's overall weakness and vulnerability with the abuser.

When the victim is aware that their family and friends are quietly whispering and asking each other why she stays in a deceptive relationship, the victim starts feeling a large amount of shame. When the victim knows deep down that they are more valuable and worthy than the messages they are accepting from the abuser. This feeling of shame even becomes bigger.. The proud person that you have learned to love and accept within, has now become enslaved to an emotional abuser. Shame alone can stop you from seeking help. Therefore, be truthful and confront this toxic relationship straight on.

Pathological Loneliness

It is hard to believe, but admitting that you are fearful of being lonely is another reason for an addictive relationship. Admitting loneliness can also be embarrassing because it suggests that no one sees you as being worthy to love or to be around. To admit that you want companionship, when you don't have it, is a very hard and transparent statement to admit. It is not surprising that many victims stay in their toxic relationship so that they won't be lonely. They don't want to come home to an empty house. They want to be able to go on vacation with someone besides their mother. And Often times they just want to be in the club of people that can say that they have a significant other.

Food for thought, as a society, we tend to clump loneliness into the same exact spot for everyone. It is important that we to realize that there are many types of loneliness. That some loneliness is normal and should be expected as we live from day to day.

Pathological Loneliness is more serious and dangerous than the fear of loneliness. This is one of the leading indicators that you are in a toxic relationship. You have finally become aware that the relationship is toxic and you know that it is best to end the relationship. So, after hitting rock bottom, you build up the courage to leave and block all contact. This is when pathological loneliness begins.

You realize that you are by yourself and the withdrawals begin because you are still emotionally and mentally bonded to that person. This is unlike any other suffering. I know the feeling all too well; it was as a hole in my soul and a bone aching emptiness.

Many never make it through the pathological loneliness process and the pain of the withdrawals is one of the leading factors to why we open the door again to the toxic relationship. Due to the withdrawals, we call or text all because we want a hit of the relationship. Does this terminology sound familiar to a drug addict? It is very similar because recovering heroin users will tell me within my field that the hardest part is not to stop using the drug. The most difficult challenge is overcoming the sickness of the withdrawal. As the heroin users are weaning off the drug, they become so sick from coming down, to the point that they return to the heroin, not for the high, but to keep from getting sick—all in hopes to remove the withdrawal pain.

If you really want to begin to heal, the withdrawal process is something you must fight through. From experience, I can promise you that it gets better. However, if you don't get through the withdrawal process then you will never leave the toxic bondage. You're either going to die in it or be determined to break free and live.

Triggers

While undergoing the withdrawal process, there will also be triggers. These are the innocent things that reminds us of our former flame and sometimes cause us to relapse within the process of remaining free. Being that there is still a psychological attachment that will take time to remove, you will be triggered by interacting with a thing that is most commonly associated with that person. For example, say that he drove a black truck. Being so, when you see a black truck driving along, it triggers thoughts of him. A trigger can also be another person wearing the smell of their cologne. This can happen when you pass by a particular place that you two ate. Even worse is when you hear their actual voice on the voicemail.

Yes, triggers can happen to men as well. A guy shared with me that he was triggered back to a toxic relationship over seeing this woman's Facebook profile picture. He admitted that she was looking good and triggered him to reach out. He explained that he was quickly reminded why the relationship was toxic and the importance of keeping his guard up even against triggers. He explained that for guys that this can also be a social media picture, smelling her particular perfume or even seeing another person wear her favorite dress. Beware of the triggers!

Was it Really that Bad?

It's amazing that once we finally find a way out, our stimulating triggers begin to forget the lows of the toxic relationship. Yes, his voice sounds so sexy on that voicemail and we have to admit that it has put a grin on our face. We begin to have selective memory and ask ourselves, "Was it really that bad?" This is how we find ourselves not making it through the withdrawal process. We begin to have selective memory—all while magnifying the stimulating times and compressing and justifying the many abusing encounters.

This reminds me of when Moses led the nation of Israel out of Egypt. Once they were within the wilderness (a place of withdrawal) they quickly began to want to return to their abusive Oppressor (Pharaoh). For examples, after Moses had delivered them, after some struggles, they wanted to appoint a new leader and go back to Egypt. (Numbers 14:4) Besides, at least Pharaoh kept a roof over our heads. In today's terminology we say things like, "Well at least he kept the bills paid." For some, it is possible to go back due to the economic withdrawal. Yes, you had the courage to leave, but the pressure of the bills, and doing it on your own, can cause the temptation of the financial security you left behind. Oh how quickly do we forget how Pharaoh was having us make bricks with no straw.

The story of Moses reminds me of Herriot Tubman. She freed many slaves; but believe it or not, because of the fear of the unknown, there were many slaves who did not want to be free. For those who are in a toxic relationship, this is why when the way of escape is open to us, we still choose to remain in the bondage. Concerning the point of withdrawal process, while Herriot was freeing slaves, when the way got hard, there were fleeing slaves that wanted to go back. Believe it or not, but Herriot would pull a gun on them and make them keep going. Braking free from a toxic relationship is the fight of your life!

Six Dangerous Signs that You are in a Toxic Relationship

1. When your mate does not want you to prosper and succeed. If the relationship is dangerous there is a definite concern from your mate that you know your place and that your confident stays low and bruised. There is a constant reminder from them that you need them and that you can't succeed on your own.

2. When you give, give, give and your mate takes, takes, takes! There is no concern about what you want and desire. Perhaps at the beginning of the relationship your mate tried to act like they wanted you to be happy. But the more you compromised your desires and did what your mate wanted; the less they became concerned about pleasing you.

3. There is a tendency for the abusive mate to have a short and impatient temper. They become less and less tolerant. The mate doesn't care what you want, say or how you feel about the matter, they want their way at all times. They tend to have temper tantrums that often increases into becoming violent.

4. There is an obvious effort from the abusive mate to keep you away from your family and friends. They only want you around them. They fear that those closes to you, will sense your unhappiness and will start asking questions. Ultimately they are concerned the truth of how they treat you will be figured out.

5. One of the things that increases fear in the victim is the tendency for their mate to be moody and unpredictable. When you are not sure what type of

temperament you will be faced from day to day, it creates anxiety, stress and fear.

To recap, when you are made to feel you can't do anything right and you are constantly being picked on, you are in a dangerous relationship. When your mate is searching for the things you do wrong instead of ways to celebrate you, your relationship is in trouble. So ask yourself, "Am I in a toxic relationship?"

CHAPTER 5: BREAKING FREE FROM A TOXIC RELATIONSHIP

My Own Breakthrough

I was quite surprised to learn that I was a codependent. It took me a while to even understand it and believe it. How can I, Dr. Rhonda be codependent? I've heard people say, "She's too pretty and smart to be codependent!" Well it's not what you look like outside but rather what you feel like on the inside, it's all emotional. Most people will look at you with judgment like something is wrong when they are also codependent themselves.

As a little girl you have been taught to get married to your prince charming and to live happily ever after. You're never taught what type of man to marry and what type of characteristics to look for. Your dream has been set and you follow it.

I fell for the false charms of my partner's behavior. I engage in wishful thinking by naïvely believing in my toxic partner promises and excuses; instead of letting his actions speak for themselves. I blinded myself thinking that he would change. Thinking that things would get better. Gladly, God doesn't allow things to happen to you for no reason. He made me strong and took me through my transformation; because it was connected to the millions of hurting men and women in this world. I was appointed, anointed, and commissioned to do this work. I will like to say, this process is not easy. If it was, then we would all be healed. You're in the fight of your life; but aren't you worth it?

First, the most important thing that you have to do is have no contact. If you have contact with them, you can't get away from the dose of poison you are being given daily. This was hardest thing I had to endure and the most challenging step within the process. After I left the toxic relationship for the last time, I had made up my mind that this was it! I don't care if I had to die trying; I was moving forward. I wasn't going back, I was tired and I was fed-up! This is where you have to get to before you make up your mind and say, "I've had enough!" You have to hit rock bottom.

They will do anything to keep you from leaving. They will start to get scared because they are losing their power. They will cry and tell you how sorry they are; only to hoover you back into the same toxic relationship. It's a cycle of madness.

I started researching and researching trying to find out what was *narcissism*. I was trying to fix him not me. What a big mistake. You can't concentrate on how to fix your mate; you have to concentrate on how to look within and heal yourself. With the guidance of God, I used a technique named *Mindfulness*. The purpose of this technique is to be present in the moment.

Mindfulness is a pretty straightforward. your mind will keep going back to the events of hurt and pain over and over. This is why we go back to the toxic relationships; thinking that I must be in love because I keep thinking about my partner. What happens is our mind takes flight, we lose touch with our body and pretty soon we're engrossed in obsessive thoughts about something and this makes us anxious. We have to be fully present, aware of where we are and what we're doing. Now believe me, it isn't easy, but well worth the battle. I'll say it again, you're in the battle of your life! If this was easy, so many of us would not be in toxic relationships. People say, "Just leave that person; you'll be okay." What they don't know is it's not that easy because it's an addiction.

I know when I went through the breaking up phase of the relationship with the narcissist. After the crumbling of the illusion of what I believed to be true, I had very little energy to do anything at all. I just wanted to lay down and sleep. This is a common state of mind we find ourselves in after ending a toxic relationship.

This is why you have to go to someone that is professionally trained in *narcissism* and *codependency*. When I was researching and trying to find someone who could help me understand why I was addicted to certain relationships, it was like pulling teeth. They wanted to charge me a $1,000 a month for a year with a contract. really! After my healing, God said to me, "Why don't you begin helping others for free? I will provide the rest."

Seven Steps to Breaking Free

1. **Saying Goodbye.** Saying goodbye was really hard for me. Letting go of the illusion that I was in love and that everything was going to be great. Especially when they keep telling you how much they love you

and crying. Trust me, don't believe it! When you realize that you are dealing with the narcissistic personality, it is important to leave the situation. Get over the ideal that you can make it better or change the person. You can't change anyone! The only one you can change is yourself. You change by refusing to allow yourself to continue to be emotionally abused. You deserve to be treated with dignity and respect.

The longer you stay in a toxic relationship, the worse it will get. Of course you'll go through the honeymoon phases that I talked about earlier, but it always goes back to being much worse than it was before. If you believe it would change, you are living in a fantasy world. You will continue to dangle until you die. Trust your intuition. Trust that you know the truth somewhere deep inside. You are a worthy individual and you have a lot to offer. You are capable of having a loving healthy relationship. Say goodbye, farewell and close the door. Don't open it again; it is your only way out!

2. **No Contact.** It has been proven that the only way to truly detach from the dark reality of the narcissist is to cut off all contact from him or her. This means no Facebook, no email and no texting. Don't allow the curiosity to control you; you must rather control the situation. It's really hard because you keep asking yourself, "Did he ever love me? How could he act like he or she worshipped the ground I walk on and then turn into someone I never knew?" I can answer that for you. The answer is don't waste your time thinking about it. They could not love you because

they don't love themselves. You must work on your self-love and your worthiness. You are worth it! Once you achieve this you will attract healthy people into your life and you will be attracted to healthy people. Remember brokenness attracts brokenness; it's time to heal and be whole. The relationship that I was in was not healthy. I had to take what I was responsible for and then give God the rest. Leave the past behind; it's time to start fresh. It's time to take back your power!

3. **Grieving.** It's okay to get angry after a toxic relationship, if we continue to shut off our feelings and sweep them under the rug, then were not being real. If we are not real with ourselves, then we cannot heal. I became very angry thinking that I've wasted so much time dealing and being in a relationship that was toxic. I knew in my gut that it wouldn't work, but I just kept staying. Listening to what I know now to be other codependents telling me you should stay and work it out. Misery loves company. I was settling because I didn't know my worth and it took too much energy to find.

It's ok to be angry for a moment, but when I speak about anger, I'm referring to the healthy expression of it. I am talking about working with the energy of anger and getting it out of your body, so you can feel a peace within. The more you deal with the anger you have been suppressing throughout the relation-ship the more peace you will feel. I started meditating daily; connecting with the wounded child inside. Another thing I did was workout, working out made me feel at peace—all while getting rid of the negative energy within.

4. **Allow Yourself to Feel.** If you have given your heart, soul and mind to someone who missed it, you're bound to feel a deep sense of loss. It doesn't matter if you don't feel he/she is worth it, you're worth it. You have experienced the death of a relationship you thought was real. Death of the flesh is a very painful thing. Crying your eyes out is a very healthy thing. It is good to release all that emotional grief. You always feel better after a cry. I couldn't wait to get home from work, once walked through the door, I would fall on my knees and cry and pray over and over. Let it out; there is healing within your tears.

I felt like I had purged poisons from deep within. It is important to allow yourself to really express your heart. It is important to be conscious of what you are feeling. This is so painful that most people abort this feeling and go and hook-up with another person; with the same brokenness and a different mask. It is imperative that you go through the process of dealing with your pain so God can heal you and then awaken your most dormant dreams. I'm so glad I did!

5. **Take Back Your Power.** In order to take back your power you have to cut the psychic cord. This cord is invisible and you can't see it, but you can sure feel it. If your energy is still merging with his/hers, then you will continue to feed on this physical relationship. It is a must that you cut that energy

cord. This is a journey, so don't be upset it if it doesn't happen overnight. It's a process if you do the work. You have to take care of yourself. Now is the time to eat right and get plenty of fresh air. It's important to read things you enjoy reading, pampering yourself with candles, good music, special treat and authentic friends.

Exercising is another important way to take care of yourself. Learning yoga, going for walks is very good for the body in releasing energy. Yoga will help me replenish good energy.

Meditating or sitting in silence as an important exercise to do on a daily basis. We get so busy within our minds that we don't give them adequate quite time. Sitting quietly in silence and focusing on your breathing is extremely beneficial to your body, mind and soul. Give yourself at least 10 minutes twice a day to be still and breathe.

6. **Writing and Journaling.** Writing in a journal is a great exercise to do on a daily basis. It helps you to get in touch with your feelings and emotions and to be in the moment. I still keep my journal above my head on my dresser. When God awakens me out of a dream, I write it down right away. When I read back, within my journal, on how I was filling years ago and where I am today, it's amazing. It's only by God's divine grace that I am where I am today!

7. **Taking the Time for You.** Now is the very best time to take care of yourself. Make yourself important. Do nice things for yourself. God had

awaken so many dreams that I had forgot about. I started writing books, I started modeling and doing speaking engagements. Remember, everyone's healing is a process and it is different for every individual. You must take time to be alone with God. You must meditate on his word daily and when it's time to meet your godly soulmate, God will let you know.

You and your soulmate will have a divine purpose and you both will know what that will be. God will give you the wisdom to discern toxic people, they use to prey on you, but now you are spotting them out. Embrace yourself fully and refuse to allow the burdens of yesterday to rob you of your life today!

Please visit <u>www.renewedhealthcare.com</u> for more information.

CITATIONS

Rosenberg, Ross. (2013). The Human Magnet Syndrome: *Why We Love People Who Hurt Us*. Eau Claire, WI: PESI Publishing and Media.

Unless otherwise noted, all Scripture quotations are from the King James Version Bible. Copyright @ 1979, 1980, 1982 by Thomas Nelson, Inc., publishers Used by permission.

Made in the USA
Monee, IL
11 November 2019